milk and money

rudi boor

13-Digit ISBN: 978-1-60433-927-7
10-Digit ISBN: 1-60433-927-6

This book may be ordered by mail from the publisher. Please include $5.99 for postage and handling. Please support your local bookseller first!

Books published by Cider Mill Press Book Publishers are available at special discounts for bulk purchases in the United States by corporations, institutions, and other organizations. For more information, please contact the publisher.

Cider Mill Press Book Publishers
"Where good books are ready for press"
PO Box 454
12 Spring Street
Kennebunkport, Maine 04046

Visit us online!
www.cidermillpress.com

Typography: Times New Roman
Image Credits: All images used under official license from Shutterstock.com.
Printed in the United States
1 2 3 4 5 6 7 8 9 0
First Edition

milk and
money

rudi boor

CIDER MILL
PRESS

BOOK
PUBLISHERS
KENNEBUNKPORT, MAINE

AN *UNAUTHORIZED* PARODY

milk and money

i did not hesitate
the day you took away my innocence
in fact
i welcomed your advances
mouths agape
fumbling
for words
our two bodies intertwined
in the back of a ford fiesta

- hatchback

the world is full of too many questions
and not enough answers
too much ignorance
and not enough knowledge
and of all the questions in the world
the one everyone asks is
what is your wifi password

an *unauthorized* parody – 5

milk and money

we smiled and danced
laughed and delighted
and you kept me tickled
with fits of laughter
and then i realized
i may have peed a little bit

i stand with my sisters
who stand with their voices
and i stand with my brothers
who stand back in awe
i stand for the world
and for all its intentions
and i stand for those
who can't stand for themselves
but mostly
i stand in the kitchen
eating cold pizza over the sink

milk and money

why don't we allow ourselves
to be fierce and proud
like every man who finds
the smallest accomplishment
a point of pride
like this morning
when he said
check it out
i picked up my clothes
well whoop-de
fucking
doo

rudi boor

they say man cannot live
on bread alone
imagine the carbs

milk and money

this hangover is killing me
i'm never drinking again
was what i said last time
yet there i was
slurping jello shots
with my cousin
and her friends
you only get married once
while wearing a plastic tiara
a penis-shaped whistle
and a sash that read
miss behaving

rudi boor

i wonder if the queen of sheba
with all her gifts and mysteries
bejeweled with fragrances
and bathed in oils
ever felt as i do now
soaking in hot waters
surrounded by flowers and candlelight
and i wonder if the queen of sheba
ever peed in the bathtub too

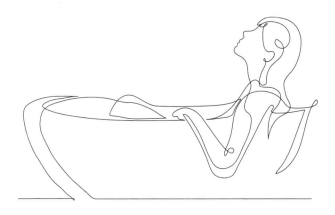

milk and money

my body is a temple
and this temple
just blew out
another pair of yoga pants

i get chills
with the touch of your hand
on my cheek
is it wrong to have a crush
on my dentist

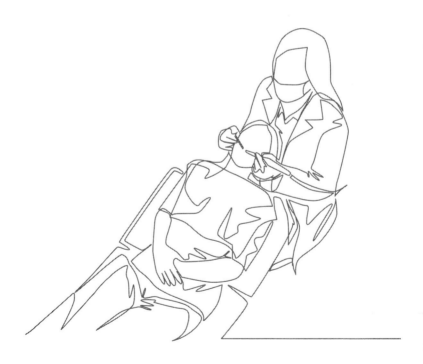

milk and money

a couple holding hands
eyes meeting longingly
in a birchbark canoe
in the dark of a cinema
in a field of sunflowers
on a train ride through the mountains
why isn't my relationship
as romantic as the one
in this erectile dysfunction drug commercial

rudi boor

we thought we could live on love alone
but i would kill
for a beef chalupa
right about now

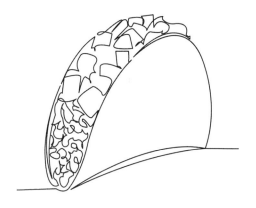

milk and money

if i could turn back time
i would tell my younger self
about the wisdom of my years
like reading more books
and less us weekly
and how that hairdo i had
sophomore year
was not artsy and european
it was just plain ugly

rudi boor

the fog of sleep sweeps from my mind
the morning sun shines on my pillow
the smell of the grass greets me
the birds chirp loudly outside my window
jesus christ
they won't stop chirping
shut up
shut up
shut the fuck up

milk and money

someday i will have a daughter
and i will teach her to be strong
and arm her with knowledge
and confidence that i never had
i will teach her to be fearless
and give her the tools to succeed
someday she will thrive
in a world of possibility
and reach new heights
that i found unattainable
and someday she will call me a bitch
on some form of social media
that hasn't been invented yet

rudi boor

he is ruggedly handsome
and i slept with him again
even though he ordered
an *espresso*
the next morning
i mean *really*

milk and money

what are our dreams
except movies of our own making
our hopes our fears our loves
projected on our sleeping minds
last night i dreamt
that a dude i knew from high school
was wearing cargo shorts
while jogging on a treadmill

rudi boor

the stroke of your fingertips
sent chills up my spine
and my hair stood on end
as you moved your hands
across my body
and under the arch of my back
your warm wet kisses
greeted me softly
and stole my breath away
with slow rhythmic panting
sweat gathering on your brow
and the communion of our bodies
you left me thinking
wait...that's it
that's not even three minutes

milk and money

the sting of the salt air
the smell of the ocean
fills my nostrils
i am never cooking shrimp
in the house again

rudi boor

i have never felt so uncertain
and i am not ashamed to tell you
that i am somewhat fearful
so please come in here
and tell me
what is that thing
sitting in the take-out container
in the back of the fridge

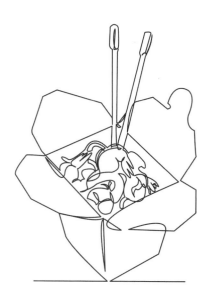

milk and money

we should get a tiny house he said
and i began to daydream
smiling at the thought
of cozy days
and intimate nights
you're so charming i said
but ain't no way
i'm living in a trailer

we must all evolve
and keep growing in our own way
taking lessons from the past
learning from our mistakes
and enjoying life's surprises
like the time
i accidentally sent a sext
to a woman in my spin class
and she replied
with a thumbs-up emoji

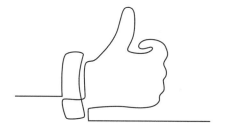

milk and money

he walks in with a purpose
and pulls up a chair
hello my sweet he says
as he sits down next to me
hello i reply
please don't cut your toenails
in the living room

rudi boor

remember that time
we went to vegas
and i drank so many margaritas
i made out with the towel boy
well i think i just saw him
on an episode of dateline

milk and money

because i am a woman
i am full of wisdom
because i am a woman
i am full of wonder
because i am a woman
my bra is killing me

we lie down in the cool grass and the stars
blanket us. the winds die down and the silence
washes over us. you reach your hand over and
interlace your fingers with mine. i hear you
breathing faintly next to me. i smile and cannot
help but think this is some kind of heaven. just
you and i and the stars. flickering playfully
above for us only. what the hell was that? no
somewhere over there behind the car. i don't
know. where's your flashlight? what do you
mean you didn't bring a flashlight? what the hell
were you thinking? i can't see a fucking thing.
now i'm going to die out here because you're an
idiot.

milk and money

my mind wanders
through lives lived
loves lost
and opportunities missed
and i ask myself
why did i think jeggings
were a good idea

rudi boor

you are an explorer
discovering my body for the first time
the mountains and valleys
the inlets and shoals
but be warned
i ran out of razors
and *here be dragons*

milk and money

i never should have told you
you look like a million bucks
because it doesn't suit you
you look like a buck fifty
and a pack of smokes

rudi boor

an old boyfriend reached out to me
and got me thinking
about old times
about lost loves
about missed opportunities
about past mistakes
about huge regrets
about time i'll never get back
about second chances
and so i replied
new phone
who dis

milk and money

if i could perform some bit of magic
and let the world see inside me
they would see
hopes and dreams
fire and passion
love and loss
and nearly a pint
of cherry garcia

rudi boor

the world conspired to put us together
lacing our paths at an unsuspecting moment
now it's you who i'm bound to
you and your ratty old couch
that smells like backsweat and old farts

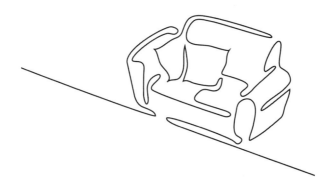

milk and money

i took the first step
and started the journey
of a thousand miles
my heart said
now is the time
he asks *why are you crying*
but i can't find the words
how can i tell him
without inventing a new language
of the heartbreak
of the last episode of the office

rudi boor

an ancient doe lay silently
besides a wooded path
having taken its final breath
and some butthole
stuck a cigarette in its mouth
like it smoked menthols

milk and money

you should love yourself
and each other
at all times
and all ways
but not
in all places

- *a used condom in a porta potty is so gross*

one day the world will see me
for who i am
what gives me meaning
my unvarnished self
the world will see my true nature
my character
and my soul
they will capture my essence
and fashion a fragrance
with a bottle shaped in my image
and the perfume will be called
lethargy

milk and money

every white flake
with its unique shape
none like the other
falls from the sky
for the love of god
get some head & shoulders

rudi boor

one should be attracted
like bees to honey
like magnets to metal
like moths to a flame
but with you it's more like
flies to a turd

milk and money

the world was alive
with the radiance of sparkling lights
millions of lives in a wildly choreographed dance
conversations over drinks
dust swept out a shop door
music climbing through a closed window
sedans rumbling down the streets
stolen kisses on subway platforms
the moon sauntering across the sky
laughing crying singing smiling
dying
falling in love
but not me
i was at home
throwing up in the sink

- bad biriyani

rudi boor

the day we met was a tuesday
on wednesday we kissed
and on thursday i fell for you
friday we made love
on saturday we skipped
right to the awkward stage
on sunday i ghosted you
stop texting me
you're gross

milk and money

loving
a man like you
brings its own pain
will you please shave
it's like kissing sandpaper

rudi boor

they said it wasn't possible
they said it couldn't happen
they said you can't
throw out your back
just sitting on the toilet
but somehow
i have done the impossible

milk and money

some days i would like
to find inspiration
open my heart to change
channel positive energy
and conquer the world
other days i would like
to take a couple percocet
and chill the fuck out

rudi boor

if spark becomes fire
and seed becomes flower
sapling becomes forest
and smoke becomes flame
what do our souls become
who gives a shit i say
sipping a dirty martini
we're all going to hell anyway

milk and money

why do you look so perplexed he asked
and i hesitated to answer
what's eating you
but i would not tell him
that i will never understand
why pumpkin spice is a thing

rudi boor

i took a path
i had never taken before
and lost myself
far from home
far from the everyday
out of my comfort
into the silence
and man
now i really have to pee

milk and money

if we could stand
on the shoulders
of our parents
and our grandparents
and look out on the world
we would be
about seventeen feet tall

rudi boor

i step outside myself
and inside myself
out of my own skin
and into my own thoughts
flesh blood sinew and synapse
blood bone emotion and ego
standing in silence
staring in mirrors
soul searching navel gazing
only to discover
there is lint in my belly button

- cheap dryer sheets

milk and money

it had been years since we'd met
and years since we'd grown apart
shared past shared memories
kept us together
diverging paths diverging lives
kept us apart
time and space
the great separation
yet here we were
together again
as it had been years ago
and fell back in the same routine
and as the cobwebs washed away
i began to realize
what a dick he was

rudi boor

i remember that spring day
of my childhood when
my mother and i walked down the street
of my old hometown
shopping for an easter dress
the old ladies
stopped to speak to my mother
and pinched me on the cheek
oh how you've grown
they said
do you like baseball
they asked
no i replied *not really*
they were surprised
then why do you have
a pete rose haircut

milk and money

we are in love with the world
and all of its magic
the wonders that make up
everyday life
serendipitous moments
and simple pleasures
which is why i'm crying
while watching a dog video
on twitter

every day i look in the mirror
and see the same person
yet over time
that person has changed
and i wonder
how the fuck
am i going to fit
into this bathing suit
come summer

milk and money

i have changed my diet
and i have sworn off pork
but i tell you this
i could definitely
go for a piece
of jon hamm

rudi boor

one day
i will not speak ill of anyone
i will not heed their caustic remarks
i will not be bothered by petty thoughts
i will be the model of restraint
and i will be at peace
because i will be dead

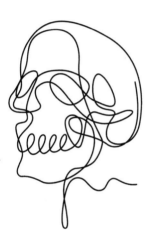

milk and money

there are certain actions
one should never take
like getting high
with your mom

rudi boor

men have let me down
and disappointed me
my entire life
but donald trump
has ruined cheetos for me
forever

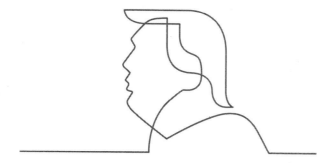

milk and money

green like your eyes
blue like my sorrow
red like your passion
yellow like my cowardice
white like your purity
black like my soul
one by one i see the colors
so where the fuck
is that other matching sock

- this drawer is a mess

rudi boor

the kindness of strangers
is the most precious gift
except for that teenage kid
sitting on the train
who offered me his seat
and called me *ma'am*
c'mon dude
i'm only thirty-four

milk and money

it has been said
when life gives you lemons
make lemonade
so what do you make
when life gives you crabs

rudi boor

whoever thought
the man bun
was a good look
deserves a serious beating

milk and money

i have taken some time for myself
to cleanse my mind and body
and heal
from the everyday stress
of the everyday world
yet here i find myself
shame eating
while watching
a trashy couple fight
on the steve harvey show

rudi boor

what scares me more than anything
is loneliness
the thought of a world as big as ours
and feeling isolated
among the billions of other people
as if not one person can relate
to how i see this world
and how i feel unseen
loneliness scares me
that and the creepy clown guy
who lives in the sewer
in that one movie
now *that* guy is freaky

milk and money

you tell me all your strategies
but seriously
what's the big deal
with super mario kart

the human brain
is a complex
and complicated
force of life
that allows you
to brush your teeth
and poop
at the same time

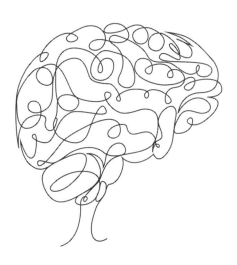

milk and money

we all need good people
in our lives
to inspire us
and keep us strong
like my best friend
with the awesome job
and killer bod
who just got engaged
and now i'm like
i'm so happy for you
bitch

rudi boor

you left me vulnerable
you left me alone
you left me naked
i'm never going
skinny dipping
with you again

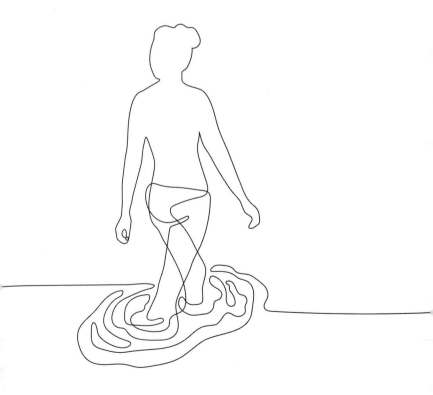

an *unauthorized* parody – 69

milk and money

you will sway with the storm
and you will bend
but you will not break
i too will bend
and scream in pain
because i have
a herniated disc
fuck my life

rudi boor

life should be simple
yet we overcomplicate things
in protecting our ego
we talk too much
why did i tell my boss
about my pelvic exam
in a long-winded oration
i am the abraham lincoln
of gynecology

milk and money

be who you want to be
to each his own
some like licorice
others like anchovies
some love avocados
others love lima beans
as for me
i say they're all wrong
that stuff is totes disgusting

your touch is soft as a lamb
your kisses sweet as honey
then you squeeze my butt
and make a sound
like an old-timey car horn
oooooo-ga

milk and money

i am cutting and clipping
the events of my life
saving and sharing
the moments that have made me
the person that i have become
and i have put these mementos
into a giant book of memories
with sweat and tears
and paper and scissors
all the while
getting a huge buzz
from huffing glue

i studied the water
as it flowed and eddied
and noticed all the hair
caught in the drain
and i thought
at this rate
i will be bald
by september

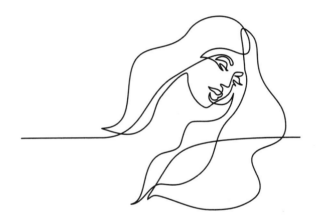

milk and money

your elegance is deceiving
as there is something weird
about the way you sneeze
like your face just suffered
a series of small explosions
and needs to be demolished

rudi boor

we can spend hours doing nothing
and yet i feel as though
we've spent a lifetime learning
to love each other
though i have to ask you
who taught you how to kiss
that thing with all the teeth
is not at all sexy

milk and money

some words remind me
of childhood
and i reflect
some words remind me
of good friends
and i laugh
some words remind me of you
and i smile
but i will never smile
at the word
moist

rudi boor

whatever you do
don't give up your dreams
and don't give in to your fears
like accidently making eye contact
with some guy in a trenchcoat
riding the m55 bus

milk and money

the sun shines on the dashboard
and lights up your face
and you shine like a diamond
as we drive through the country
and i think
how lucky am i
and then i catch you
bringing up phlegm
and spitting it out the window
like some dirt farmer
in a steinbeck novel

rudi boor

no regrets i tell myself
as i move forward
in the face of adversity
our choices make us who we are
but i simply can't ignore
that tramp stamp
i got in college

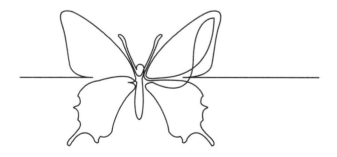

milk and money

the body is a miracle
of sinew and bone
working as one
to give you life
that said
what's with ringworm
and how did i get it

rudi boor

your flirtation
was like my first taste of champagne
i was intrigued
i was enamored
and then i threw up in my mouth

milk and money

you are like a piece of cake
that i dropped on the floor
as disgusting as you are
i will enjoy you anyway
despite my better judgement
and risk of illness

rudi boor

i am living my best life
i am making the most of every moment
i am inspired and inspiring
i don't care that i hit reply all
and told everyone at work
i was missing the meeting
because i was getting a mole removed
i am formidable
i am fierce
i will never microwave salmon
in the break room again
i am looking into the future
head held high
next time i will not explode
a toner cartridge all over
the copy room floor
and ruin my brand new white keds
because i am living my best life

milk and money

the sun bakes the leaves
grass crunches underfoot
birds hide in the boxwood
the breeze has taken a holiday
and my inner thighs are squeaking
like a bicycle tire

rudi boor

i love you
but your feet
are freezing
please put on some socks
before you come to bed

- for chrissake

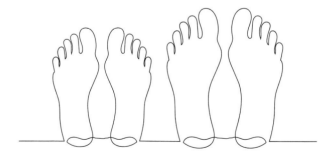

milk and money

you are an adventurous lover
and you take me to the edge
of fantasy and desire
but we need to make a rule
about strawberry sauce in bed
it looked like something
out of an episode
of csi

rudi boor

life is an education
of experiences
good and bad
i'm not sure which is worse
your dad walking in
on you naked
or you walking in
on your dad naked

milk and money

i am learning
to summon my strength
and become a badass
yesterday
i used a coupon
at bed bath and beyond
that expired six months ago

- thug life

rudi boor

the world needs laughter
which is why
i show people photos
from my junior prom
you can thank me later

an *unauthorized* parody – 91

milk and money

the way you look at me
from across the room
and the way you smile at me
as i pass you by
is giving me
douche vibes

rudi boor

a warm summer day
welcomes bees to flowers
leads birds to song
brings strength to fragrance
that stings the nose
we really should
get the septic tank pumped

- it stinks

milk and money

the lines on my face mean i'm smiling
the gray in my hair means i'm wise
the curves of my body mean i'm beautiful
and the bloating in my stomach means
i'm totally constipated

some words cannot go unspoken
some actions cannot be undone
some beliefs cannot be unchanged
and some sights cannot be unseen
like looking up hemorrhoids
on wikipedia

- *brutal*

milk and money

life is made up of everyday providence
where paths cross by chance
and people become part of your life
out of nowhere
for example judy
in the cubicle next to me
who talks too loudly on the phone
and has a laugh
that sounds like sheep being slaughtered

rudi boor

the key to happiness is love
the key to love is friendship
the key to friendship is honesty
which reminds me
where are the damn car keys

- i need an oil change

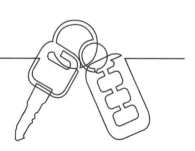

milk and money

i have seen children laughing
and lovers embrace
the flight of the eagle
and the relentless crawl of the snail
the tops of mountains
and the greatness of the ocean
but i have never seen
how one gets a zit
on the back of their neck

rudi boor

i have seen orion in the night sky
with his ornamental belt
and his club of bronze
and i have wondered
is that thing down there
supposed to be his schlong

milk and money

i think of kissing you
as i would think of
the seven wonders of the world
because i have over half a dozen questions
i've been wondering about your breath

did you think that you possess me
that i live by your beck and call
you are not my master
i do not live by your command
a boy like you should not be so vain
to think you hold sway
over a woman like me
that said
it was nice to get a booty call
and know
i still got it

milk and money

i have made the decision
not to go to work today
because i'm exhausted
and i just can't
looks like
my grandmother died
again

i may never amass a great fortune
a vast library
or a coterie of lovers
but someday
i will be known as
that crazy cat lady

milk and money

people can judge me
but they cannot change me
i am immune to their idle chitchat
they may not like it
when i wear
a big floppy beach hat
and peeky toe sandals
to synagogue
but whatevs
haters gonna hate

rudi boor

he starred in my daydreams
and haunted my nightmares
tell me what kind of person
sends a dick pic
unasked for

milk and money

why must we be paralyzed
by our decisions
we strive to examine our past
in order to empower our future
to make informed choices
based on what has been
a series of happy accidents
and incidental fortune
so what the fuck am i doing here
swipe left

you pursued me
like a lion in the serengeti
and i waited patiently
for you to pounce
and then
you asked me out
with a text message
full of eggplant emojis
i mean seriously
don't

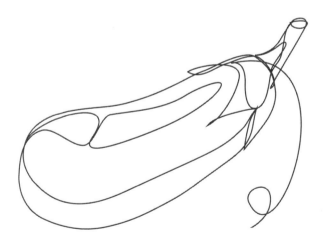

milk and money

i have a shoebox
full of wine corks
and sea shells
for an undetermined art project
that will probably never happen

rudi boor

every once in a while
i convince myself
that i'm a hat girl
and then it turns out
i'm really not a hat girl

milk and money

you are only as old as you feel
and i refuse to act my age
and then i noticed
some gray pubes
in the shower
and i thought *gee*
thanks god
for the reminder

you are a strong woman
who can climb mountains
and run marathons
but what a waste of a sunday
when you could be outside
downing a few mimosas
and eating eggs florentine
with hollandaise on the side

milk and money

he was a mystery
and i searched for the answer
we sent cryptic messages
and spoke in hushed tones
we revealed ourselves
and made secret plans
we agreed on a time
and a place
and a date
and then
i had to send up the bat signal
for my friend to call me
with an emergency
during the salad course
because he was a weirdo
and there was no way
i could make it
to dessert
with that douchebag

your hand on my shoulder
reveals your dark secret
your playful gesture
your sideways glance
gives you away
pursed lips nonchalance
uncomfortable smile
curtailed emotion
an innocent laugh
the warm breeze on my face
tells the truth

- stop farting

milk and money

is it wrong to fall in love
with the wrong person
isn't *love* the point
and if it *is love*
then is it wrong
because i just met
a hot dude
who delivered my papa john's

rudi boor

children are a miracle
innocent and unafraid
full of life
and full of curiosity
like the kid at target
who said
hey lady
are you pregnant

milk and money

today i got a surprise
in my mailbox
it was a postcard
from my doctor
i'm due for a mammogram

- *hurray*

rudi boor

for the child in me
the circus never ends
the world is an amazing place
full of curiosity
wonder and laughter
but the adult in me
wants this carnival
to be over soon
cause i got the bed spins
like a fucking merry-go-round

milk and money

i am trying to release myself
from the trappings of a material world
and let go of those possessions
that are weighing me down
but i have over twenty scarves
i will never wear
and i'm keeping them
cause they're really cute
and i could look amazeballs
like audrey hepburn or something

rudi boor

to truly be in love
one must suffer for the other
we give ourselves over
feeling the pain that comes
from loving another person
like me getting scratched
by my zipper
while dry humping

milk and money

damn
i muttered
as i opened
my paycheck

rudi boor

his was a generous love
which gave me everything i asked for
he was gentle and supportive
and warm and welcoming
he was unselfish
and selfless enough
to satisfy me alone
his was a generous love
and then his generosity ended
and he fell asleep and
left me laying in the wet spot

milk and money

we all have small secrets
that keep the wheels of society
turning in the right direction
which is why i ate
a small hunk of cheese
back in the bedroom
so my roommate wouldn't see
and be all judgey

rudi boor

do not tempt me
with your sugar-coated language
just because you call them
progressive lenses
doesn't hide the fact
i now wear bifocals

milk and money

i will never know what it means
to act like a man
or what it's like to live
inside of a masculine body
but i have seen enough skidmarks
to know it must be gross

rudi boor

sometimes i think
we are antony and cleopatra
but if i'm being honest
we're really just
liz lemon and dennis

milk and money

what the hell is going on here
if the world is your oyster
then i got shucked hard.

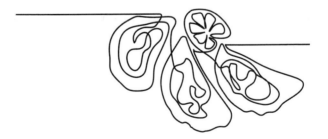

126 – an *unauthorized* parody

rudi boor is not a bestselling author and has illustrated nothing since middle school. her poetry collection is entirely parody and offers no new insights into the complexity of anything. rudi views her life as a journey to the next margarita bar, and her poems deal with shame, one-night stands, and trashy decision making, because that's really all life is anyway. once, after dropping out of college, rudi read her poetry at an empty bar and the lack of booing inspired her to share her work with the world.

- *about the writer*

About Cider Mill Press Book Publishers

Good ideas ripen with time. From seed to harvest, Cider Mill Press brings fine reading, information, and entertainment together between the covers of its creatively crafted books. Our Cider Mill bears fruit twice a year, publishing a new crop of titles each spring and fall.

"Where Good Books Are Ready for Press"

Visit us online:
www.cidermillpress.com

Or write to us at
PO Box 454
12 Spring St.
Kennebunkport, Maine 04046